Gandhi

JANE ROLLASON

Level 2

Series Editors: Andy Hopkins and Jocelyn Potter

Pearson Education Limited
Edinburgh Gate, Harlow,
Essex CM20 2JE, England
and Associated Companies throughout the world.

ISBN: 978-1-4058-7693-3

First published by Penguin Books 2004
This edition first published by Pearson Education 2008

14

Typeset by Graphicraft Ltd, Hong Kong
Set in 11/14pt Bembo
Printed in China
SWTC/14

Published by Pearson Education Ltd.

Acknowledgements
The publisher would like to thank the following for their kind permission to reproduce their photographs:
(Key: b-bottom; c-centre; l-left; r-right; t-top)
3 akg-images Ltd: Archiv Peter Rühe (b). **Getty Images:** Henry Guttmann / Stringer (t). 5
TopFoto: Topham Picturepoint. 7 **Getty Images:** Keystone-France \ Gamma-Rapho. 12 **Getty
Images:** Keystone. 13 **Getty Images:** Popperfoto. 16 **akg-images Ltd:** Archiv Peter Rühe /
Copyright: GandhiServe. 17 **Getty Images:** Popperfoto. 19 **TopFoto:** ullsteinbild. 23 **Getty
Images:** Keystone
Cover images: *Front:* **Getty Images:** Bettmann; *Back:* **Getty Images:** Bettmann
All other images © Pearson Education

*Every effort has been made to trace the copyright holders and we apologise in advance for any unintentional omissions.
We would be pleased to insert the appropriate acknowledgement in any subsequent edition of this publication.*

For a complete list of the titles available in the Pearson English Readers series, visit
www.pearsonenglishreaders.com.
Alternatively, write to your local Pearson Education office or to Pearson English Readers
Marketing Department, Pearson Education, Edinburgh Gate, Harlow, Essex CM20 2JE, England.

Contents

Introduction

Gandhi looked at the ocean and walked onto the beach. He took some salt in his hand and showed it to the people. "I am breaking the law," he said.

Gandhi was an ordinary boy from an ordinary Hindu family in India. He married and had children. He studied law at college in England. But he was not an ordinary man.

His first job took him to South Africa. Here life was hard for Indians. They were not Christians and they were not white. A policeman threw Gandhi off a train because of his color. This changed him. He started to fight for the rights of Indians.

When Gandhi left India in 1893, he wore European clothes. He came back to India in 1915 in simple, white Indian clothes. This was a different man—a man with ideas and new ways of protest.

In India, Gandhi started to fight for independence from Britain. It took more than thirty years. He wanted to change India's rulers. But he also wanted to change Indians. He showed them a simple, holy way of life.

When an angry Hindu shot Gandhi, for a minute a light went out in the world. "But," said Jawaharlal Nehru, the first leader of free India, "in a thousand years, people will see that light . . . It is the light of truth."

Mahatma Gandhi is famous everywhere in the world. He died in 1948, but everybody knows his name. He was an Indian leader, but he was also a world leader. He showed the world nonviolent protest. People in many countries follow his ideas today.

Chapter 1   An Ordinary Boy
(1869–1881)

Mohandes Karamchand Gandhi was born in 1869 in Porbandar, in the west of India. His family were Hindus. Most Indians are Hindus, and Gandhi came from an ordinary Hindu home. They weren't a poor family and he went to school. He read books and he played in the streets with his friends. He hated sports at school, but he enjoyed long walks.

"I made mistakes when I was young," Gandhi wrote later. One day he took some money from his older brother's room. He felt bad about that.

Another time, he didn't listen to his mother. "Hindus never eat meat or fish. They never kill animals," she always told him. But his friend had different ideas. He told Gandhi, "The British are strong because they eat meat. They rule India because they are strong." So Gandhi ate meat, but he didn't tell his mother.

He lived an ordinary life and he made ordinary mistakes. But he wasn't an ordinary man. He was a Mahatma, a "Great Soul," and a leader of his people.

◆

When Gandhi was born, Britain was a strong country. It ruled India. How did this happen?

1497   The first Europeans arrived in India by ship. They were Portuguese. The Dutch, British, and French followed. At this time, India wasn't one country—it had many different leaders.

1600   The British started the East India Company. They wanted to buy things from India. They gave money to some leaders and killed other leaders. They fought the Dutch and French in India, too.

1757   An Indian ruler, Siraj-ud-Daula, fought the British. The French helped him, but the British won.

1818   The East India Company ruled most of India. Clothes, sugar, and other things went from India to Britain by ship.

1857   Indians fought the British everywhere in India. The British won, but they closed the East India Company. There was now a British ruler in India. He had 70,000 British soldiers and 160,000 Indian soldiers.

1899   By this time India, Canada, Australia, Hong Kong, Singapore, Jamaica, South Africa, and other places in Africa were all in the British Empire. The British bought and sold things. They made a lot of money from their empire.

1900   Many British people were born and died in India. It was their home. But they didn't live with Indians—they ruled them. Some richer Indians went to Britain. They studied there. Poorer Indians went to other places in the Empire and worked there.

Chapter 2   "Coloreds sit in third class!" (1882–1915)

Mohandes was only thirteen when his parents found a wife for him. Her name was Kasturbai and she was thirteen, too. At that time, most Hindus married when they were very young. Mohandes and Kasturbai had their first child in 1886.

Gandhi went to London at the age of eighteen. His mother didn't like the idea. "How can you be a good Hindu in London?" she asked. But he wanted to study law.

When he first arrived in Britain, he wanted to be an Englishman. He took dancing lessons and he dressed in European clothes. But he didn't feel right. He thought about Kasturbai and their baby at home in India. His English wasn't good. London was an expensive city. He didn't like the food and usually it was meat.

"I'm not British, I'm Indian," he thought. "I'll move to a cheaper room. I'll walk everywhere. Then I can live on very little money." He felt happier. He worked hard at college for three years. Then he went back to India. He was a lawyer.

Gandhi, a student in London   *Gandhi's wife, Kasturbai*

Gandhi's first important job was in South Africa. He took a ship from Bombay to Durban in 1893. He was sad because he had to leave Kasturbai again. But he was excited about the work and it was only for one year.

South Africa was also under British rule. Many Indians lived there, but the white rulers didn't like them. They called them "colored." They made different laws for Indians and black Africans.

A month after he arrived, something happened to Gandhi. It changed him.

One evening in 1893 Gandhi was on a train from Durban to Pretoria. He was in first class. The train stopped at Petermaritzburg in Natal. A white man got on the train and saw Gandhi.

"Get out of here. Coloreds can't sit in here," he shouted at him.

"But I have a first class ticket," protested Gandhi. "I am a lawyer. In England I always sit in first class."

"There are no colored lawyers in South Africa," said the white man. He called a policeman.

"Move to third class," said the policeman. "Or get off the train."

Gandhi didn't move, so the policeman threw him off the train. Then he threw his bags off. Gandhi stayed the night at Petermaritzburg station. The night was long and cold. He thought about the white man. He and the other man were different colors—but they were only men. He thought for hours: "I can help the Indians here. I can stay and fight. Or I can go back to India."

Gandhi stayed in South Africa for the next twenty years.

In 1896 Gandhi brought his family to South Africa. He read a lot of books. He wanted to learn new ideas. He wanted to change things. He read the holy books of Muslims, Christians, and Hindus—the Koran, the Bible, and the Bhagavad Gita. He read Plato, Tolstoy, and John Ruskin, an English writer. "A good life is a simple life," Ruskin wrote. "Hard work is good for our souls. People only want things because other people have them." When

Gandhi, a lawyer in South Africa

Gandhi liked an idea, he followed it. He liked these ideas and he changed his life. In 1904 he started his first *ashram** near Durban.

Many Indians in South Africa lived in Natal and Transvaal. Here they worked on sugar and coffee farms. Some richer Indians had companies, but most Indians were poor. South Africa had hard laws for Indians and black Africans. "We will never be the same as whites

* *ashram*: a simple farm. A lot of people live there, without a leader. Each person does every job.

here," Gandhi knew. "But we can change some things." He started a newspaper for Indians.

Then things got worse. In 1907 there was a new law in Transvaal. Indians there had to carry new papers. The South African police could go into an Indian house and ask for these papers. Indians without papers went to prison. They called it the "Black Law." This law gave Gandhi a new idea.

Gandhi called a meeting and many Indians came. The police came, too. In front of the police, Gandhi put his papers in a fire. They took him to prison. Gandhi wanted to go to prison. His new idea was nonviolent protest. "We say 'no' to this law, but we will never use violence," he said. "We are right and they are wrong. The truth will make us strong."

Harder laws came next. Under these new laws, only Christians could marry in South Africa. Muslims and Hindus couldn't marry, and most Indians there and in India were Hindus or Muslims. Indian workers also couldn't move freely around South Africa.

When Gandhi came out of prison, he started another nonviolent protest. In October 1913 he marched with thousands of Indians from Natal into Transvaal. They walked without shoes and they ate only bread and sugar. The police stopped the march, and Gandhi went to prison again. A lot of other Indians went to prison, too. Many more people stopped work. The South African police hit the Indians, but the Indians didn't fight them.

Gandhi and his nonviolent protest were famous. His picture was often in the Indian newspapers because of his protests in South Africa. The world waited. This time the protest worked. In 1914 South Africa changed its laws. Everybody could marry.

Gandhi now turned to the question of independence for India. "I can do more at home," he thought. With Kasturbai and their children—now four sons—he left Johannesburg in July 1914. First, they went to England. Gandhi was forty-five. A month later, World War 1 (1914–18) started.

Chapter 3   "Go and find India!"
(1915–1919)

Gandhi and Kasturbai arrived back in India in 1915. Many people met the ship. They shouted Gandhi's name. Then they saw a small, thin man in simple, white Indian clothes. Indian leaders usually wore expensive European clothes. "Is that Gandhi?" they asked. "He's very short. And what's he wearing?"

Gandhi was famous in his country, but he didn't know his country very well. An old Indian friend and teacher said to him,

Gandhi and his wife, in India again

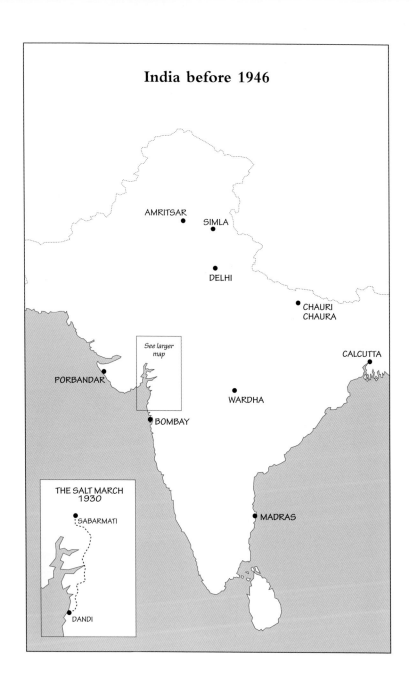

India before 1946

AMRITSAR

SIMLA

DELHI

CHAURI
CHAURA

*See larger
map*

CALCUTTA

PORBANDAR

WARDHA

BOMBAY

THE SALT MARCH
1930

SABARMATI

MADRAS

DANDI

"Go and find India! Listen, but do not speak. Learn!"

Gandhi went to many different places in India and he met thousands of ordinary people. He went everywhere by train. He always sat in third class because he remembered South Africa.

A famous Indian writer and holy man, Tagore, had a school. Gandhi met him there in 1915 when he visited the school. The students played music and danced. They wore flowers and they didn't do much work. Life at the school was beautiful. Tagore gave his new friend a new name—"Mahatma Gandhi."

After a year, Gandhi talked to Indian leaders. "Wear Indian clothes—make jobs for Indians," he told them. "Meet ordinary people. Speak *their* languages, not English. They don't understand English. They live in the country and they are poor. They don't go to school. We want to change India. First we have to understand the country and know the people."

Gandhi started an ashram next to the Sabarmati River, near Ahmedabad. Money for the ashram came from rich families in Bombay and Ahmedabad. At the beginning, about thirty people lived there. Later, there were 230. Gandhi wanted to show India a simple way of life without machines.

There were many Hindus in India. But not all Hindus were the same. There were different classes. In the highest class were the holy men. Then there were the soldiers. Next came the farmers—this was Gandhi's class. And at the bottom, there were "Untouchables." They did the dirty jobs. They cleaned the streets. Other Hindus didn't want to talk to Untouchables.

Gandhi invited a family of Untouchables to the ashram. "Come and live with us," he said to them. "I would like your daughter to be my daughter." Kasturbai was angry. "They go or I go," she protested. "You go, then," answered Gandhi. "We are all children of God. Life for Untouchables in India is as bad as life for Indians in South Africa. But we can change their lives." Kasturbai stayed.

Gandhi fought for many things in his life. In India he wanted five things: no violence between Hindus and Muslims; the same rights for Untouchables as for other Hindus; Indians in Indian clothes; the same rights for women as for men; independence for India from British rule.

Chapter 4 "I wanted to teach India a lesson." (1919–1922)

Many Indian soldiers fought with Britain in World War 1 and many gave their lives. When the war ended in 1918, Indian leaders thought, "Now the world is changing. The British will give us more rights." But they were wrong. In 1919 Britain made worse laws for Indians.

"India can never win independence!" people said.

"Nothing is impossible," answered Gandhi. He thought hard about the problem. One morning he woke up with a new idea: a "no-work day." On a no-work day, everybody stays at home and fasts. Stores, schools, and offices close. Trains don't run.

Gandhi called a no-work day across India. People loved it. They felt strong. Everything stopped for 24 hours. But there was some violence. Some people weren't ready for nonviolent protest.

In the town of Amritsar in the Punjab, the British wanted to stop the protest. They put two Indian leaders in prison on April 11, 1919. People were angry. They ran through the streets and killed two British bank workers. When Dyer, an important British soldier in the Punjab, heard about this, he was very angry. "There will be no more meetings in Amritsar," he said on April 12. "No meetings, no protests, and no marches." But not everybody in Amritsar heard Dyer's words. A black day in the story of British India followed.

Many Indians in Amritsar went to a meeting in a square in the town. One man remembered later:

"Do you know Jallianwala Bagh in Amritsar? We often meet there. It's a square with a wall and buildings all around it. There's only one small road into the square. And some doors, but they weren't open on this day.

"We were there on April 13. There were a lot of us—almost 20,000 people. I was there with my brother. A man stood up on a box. He started to talk to us about protest.

"Then Dyer arrived in the square. He had about 100 soldiers with him. Everybody went quiet. Then people started to move away, first slowly and then more quickly.

"Suddenly they started to shoot. They didn't shoot over our heads. They shot *at* us. Men and women shouted. They ran. They fell. Children cried. I wanted to get out of the square, but the walls were high. Nobody could open the doors. My brother climbed on my back and they shot him. I will never forget it."

Dyer's soldiers shot 1,516 men, women, and children in ten minutes. They killed 379 people. "I wanted to teach India a lesson," he said.

"We will not work with these people," Gandhi said after Amritsar. In 1920 he started a new nonviolent protest. He went around India and talked to people. "Don't wear British clothes," he said. "We can make clothes in India. We want jobs." People took off their British clothes and threw them onto a big fire.

People were excited. "Something is going to happen," they thought. In 1922 there was a march in the small town of Chauri Chaura in the east of India. It started quietly. Then Indian police started to hit some people at the back of the march. Other marchers ran after the police and killed them. Gandhi heard about it three days later. He didn't want this to happen. He stopped the protest. But the British in India and in London were unhappy about Gandhi and his nonviolent protest. "We think he is waiting. We think he will use violence when he is ready."

In March 1922 they sent Gandhi to prison again. Gandhi didn't hate prison. He could think and read there. He stayed in prison for two years.

Police stopping protesters

Chapter 5   "I can't get away from people!" (1923–1927)

There were many more Hindus than Muslims in India at this time. There were no big problems between them in the country. But in the cities it was different. Many, many people lived in India's cities. There weren't many jobs. Most children couldn't go to school. In the long, hot summers, people got excited and angry. There was often violence between Hindus and Muslims.

Gandhi's home at the Sabarmati ashram

"It is easier for us when the Hindus hate the Muslims," the British thought. So they sometimes gave better jobs to Muslims. This made Hindus angry. Gandhi said to the Hindus, "We have to work *with* Muslims. They are our brothers. We are one family." But in 1924 the violence got worse.

Gandhi started to fast. "I will eat again when the violence stops. Not before," he said. On Day 21 of the fast, Hindu and Muslim leaders came to him. "Please stop," they said to him. "We are not fighting." Gandhi won.

He went around India again and he spoke to thousands of people. Often he went to many meetings in different places in one day. People loved him because he was the Mahatma—the soul of India. "I cannot get away from people when I am taking my bath!" he said. Often he felt very tired. He ate little and he worked hard. So for one year—1926—he stopped his meetings. He stayed at home on the Sabarmati ashram.

A writer from a magazine came to the ashram. Her readers wanted to know about life there. She asked one of Gandhi's friends some questions:

Is life hard on the ashram?

Yes. The day starts at half past four in the morning. We have to wash and dress by five o'clock. Then we think about God and read holy books for half an hour. Breakfast is after that.

What do you have for breakfast?

Fruit, usually. Next, we do the farm work. We carry water, cook, make clothes. We wash clothes and clean. Everybody does every job.

Do you have time for study?

Yes, we have school in the morning for two hours and again after lunch for three hours.

What do you study?

Languages. We learn Indian languages—Gujarati, Hindi, and Tamil, and the old language of Sanskrit.

There are a lot of children here. Are they happy?

They love it here. They love Gandhi and he loves them. He plays with them every day. They are always laughing with him.

Are there a lot of visitors?

Oh, yes, we have many visitors. They come from many countries. They all want to see Gandhi. They can come in the evening. We are asleep by ten o'clock.

Gandhi's ashram rules

1 We always tell the truth.
2 We never kill or hurt any person or animal.
3 We eat only when we are hungry.
4 We do not want many things.
5 We only wear Indian clothes.
6 We are not afraid of anything.
7 We speak Indian languages.
8 Nobody is Untouchable.

Chapter 6   "We have to do something big." (1928–1932)

The three most important Indian leaders were Gandhi, Jawaharlal Nehru, and Mohammed Ali Jinnah. Nehru was very close to Gandhi and loved him very much. He wore Indian clothes and lived a simple life. Jinnah led the Muslims. He was very different from Gandhi. He lived a European way of life and he didn't like Gandhi's ideas. He never called Gandhi "Mahatma."

These three men met British leaders in 1928. They wanted to talk about independence. But the British weren't ready for independence—they wanted to stay in India.

"We have to do something big," said Gandhi. He thought for a long time and talked to many people. And then he had an idea.

India is a hot country. Life without salt isn't possible. There is ocean to the west, south, and east of India and there is salt on the beaches. But at that time people had to pay money to the British when they took salt. "This law hurts poor people more than rich people," thought Gandhi.

He made plans. People heard about his plans and many people came to the Sabarmati ashram. There were writers from newspapers around the world. "What's he going to do?" they asked. Everybody waited.

At half past six in the morning on March 12, 1930, with seventy-eight men and women from the ashram, Gandhi started to walk to Dandi, a small place by the Indian Ocean. (See the map on page 8.) They walked twenty kilometers every day. Thousands of people stood by the road and shouted Gandhi's name. Indians everywhere listened to their radios. "We are marching in the name of God," said Gandhi. They called it the "Salt March."

Gandhi was 61. "This walk is no problem for me," he said. It was more difficult for some of the younger marchers. The march

15

The Salt March

arrived at Dandi on April 6. Gandhi looked at the ocean and walked onto the beach. He took some salt in his hand and showed it to the people. "I am breaking the law," he said.

Indians around the country went to the ocean and took salt. They sold it in the cities, but they didn't pay any money to the British. They broke the law. The police put thousands of them in prison. Nehru and other leaders went to prison for six months. Four weeks later there were 100,000 people in prison. On May 5 the British put Gandhi in prison. "Good," he thought, "Now I can get some sleep."

In the eyes of the world, the British looked stupid after the Salt March. Prison wasn't the answer. They couldn't rule India without the help of the Indians. In 1931 the British invited

"Little man" leaves London

December 5, 1931

Mr. M. K. Gandhi leaves London today after a visit of three months. This "little man" won the love of the British people. He met British leaders. He spoke at meetings and met important British and Indian people. He met workers and stayed in ordinary British homes. He did not want to stay in expensive hotels.

But there is no end to the problem of India. We do not want to lose India, but Indians want independence from us.

Gandhi to London for talks.

When Gandhi arrived back in India, things were worse. A new British leader brought in new laws. He stopped meetings and nonviolent protest. Nehru was in prison again. A month after his visit to London, Gandhi was in prison, too.

Chapter 7   "I will only eat when the violence ends." (1932–1947)

In 1932 Gandhi began a new fast in prison for the rights of Untouchables. Nehru was angry with his friend. "Why is he fasting now?" he thought. "It will not help." And then he understood. Gandhi was the Mahatma. He was the closest thing to God in the world of men. When he fasted, all India stopped. India listened to him. Indians everywhere fasted with Gandhi on the first day. Nobody went to the movies or to restaurants. And they answered his call. Holy places opened their doors to Untouchables for the first time in 3,000 years. Hindu women ate food from the hands of Untouchables. Hindu children sat next to Untouchable children in school.

In 1933 Gandhi left the fight for independence for a time. He left it to Nehru and Jinnah, and worked for the rights of poor people. He gave the Sabarmati ashram to some Untouchables and in 1936 he started a new ashram in Wardha, a little town in the center of India. He went around India on foot. He slept under trees and talked to people about their lives.

Gandhi's ideas for change were often about small things. He wanted to teach poor people about good, simple food. He wanted clean water for everybody and schools for all children. "There will always be rich people. There will always be poor people," he thought. "But in India there is a great mountain between them. It is very high." He read Karl Marx, but he didn't like his ideas. He wanted change to come from inside people, not from rulers or big ideas. He took ideas from everywhere. "I am a Christian, and a Hindu, and a Muslim, and a Jew," he said. But he always followed his idea of truth. For Gandhi, truth was God.

And then, in 1939, World War 2 (1939–45) started. Nobody listened to Gandhi's ideas about nonviolent protest this time. Other Indian leaders had different ideas. "India will fight with you,"

Gandhi and Nehru

they said to Britain, "and then you will give us independence." By 1942 the war was close to India. Japanese soldiers were in Singapore, to the east. The Germans were in Egypt, to the west. In March of that year a letter from the British leader, Winston Churchill, arrived in Delhi. "You can have independence," it said, "after the war." Churchill didn't really mean it. He didn't want to lose India.

"Leave India now," Gandhi answered. "We want to be free today, not tomorrow." He called a nonviolent protest across India. The next day Gandhi was in prison again, with Kasturbai, and other Indian leaders.

In 1944 Kasturbai was suddenly very sick. They brought her to Gandhi in prison and she died in his arms. "What is my life without her?" asked Gandhi. "She was my wife for 62 years." Kasturbai always followed her husband and worked hard for his ideas. But she died before India was free.

After the end of the war, in 1945, there were new leaders in Britain. They didn't want a British Empire; they wanted an independent India. Indian leaders met in Simla, in the north of the country.

"Independence will come now," Indians said. "It will be easy." But there was no easy way. One of the worst times for India now began. Nehru and Gandhi wanted one India. Jinnah, the Muslim leader, wanted two Indias—a Hindu India and a Muslim Pakistan. Gandhi and Jinnah talked for many hours. "You will have to cut me in two before you cut my country in two," Gandhi said. But he couldn't change Jinnah's plans.

Nehru didn't want to fight Jinnah. For him war between Muslims and Hindus was worse than two Indias. Nehru and Gandhi had to say yes to Jinnah. It was the most important fight of Gandhi's life and he lost it. "There will be two countries—India and Pakistan," said the leaders. "India will give Pakistan money," said Gandhi. "They cannot build a new country without our help." Many Hindus weren't happy with this. "Gandhi loves Muslims more than us," they said.

Violence between Hindus and Muslims began in the winter of 1946. Gandhi went to the center of the worst violence in Bengal. He walked eighteen hours a day and visited forty-nine small towns. He listened to people's stories. He was seventy-seven and it was dangerous. Some Hindus hated him now. They put glass on the roads and he cut his feet.

♦

August 15, 1947. After ninety years of the British Empire, India won independence. Indian colors—orange, white, and green—flew over Delhi. The red, white, and blue colors of Britain came down. Jawaharlal Nehru spoke to the people. He was the first leader of free India. "Long live Mahatma Gandhi!" cried the people. But Gandhi wasn't there. He was in Calcutta and he wasn't happy. He thought about the Hindu-Muslim problem, not about independence. "This is a dangerous time for our country," he thought. "There will be a lot of violence."

12,000,000 Indians had to leave their homes. Muslims went to West Pakistan (now Pakistan) and East Pakistan (now Bangladesh); Hindus went to the new India. They were angry. Many of them lost everything. There was war between them. Men, women, and children died. India won Home Rule with nonviolent protest, but where was nonviolence now?

Things were worst in Calcutta. Gandhi went there and started a fast. "I will eat again when the violence stops," he said. On the third day it stopped. Fifty thousand soldiers couldn't stop the violence, but one little old man could. At the age of seventy-eight he was the Mahatma, and people listened to him.

There was violence in Delhi, too. Gandhi went there next. He began to fast on January 13, 1948. The violence slowly stopped. He took his first drink of orange on January 18.

Chapter 8   "Oh God!"
(January 1948)

It was ten past five on the afternoon of January 30, 1948. Gandhi was in Delhi on his way to a meeting. Five hundred people waited for him. He was ten minutes late and he hated being late. He walked through the people, but one man didn't move back. The man stood in front of Gandhi.

He pulled a gun from his shirt and then he shot Gandhi three times. "Oh God!" said Gandhi, and he fell to the ground. He was dead.

The man's name was Nathuram Godse. He was a poor man, a Hindu. He didn't want two Indias and he was angry with Gandhi. "Why didn't Gandhi fight Jinnah?" he thought. "Why did he give Pakistan money? I will kill Gandhi, and the Muslims will lose their friend."

At six o'clock Nehru spoke to India on the radio. "Everywhere is dark. Our leader, the Father of our country, is dead. We will not see him again. But always remember this. A light shines in our country. It is no ordinary light...in a thousand years, people will see that light...It is the light of truth."

All night Gandhi's family sat by him. They read holy books. They cried. Thousands of people stood outside the house. They wanted to see Gandhi, and the family brought him out.

The next day two hundred soldiers took Gandhi to the Jumna River. Nehru and other leaders were there, and 2,000,000 other people watched. They put Gandhi on a fire. Ramdas, one of his sons, lit the fire.

Ordinary people around the world listened to their radios and felt very sad.

"Why do we feel sad?" people asked. "We didn't know Gandhi. We don't know India." But Gandhi was a good man and there aren't many really good men. His life was holy but never quiet. He always fought at the center of things.

Soldiers took Gandhi to the Jumna River.

Martin Luther King, Nelson Mandela, and the Dalai Lama read his books and studied his life. They used his ideas in their independence protests. Many people now follow Gandhi's ideas. Gandhi didn't win every fight. Some of his ideas didn't work. But he always followed his truth. And the light of his truth shines for many people today.

Gandhi left few things when he died.

ACTIVITIES

Chapters 1–2

Before you read

1 Look at the Word List at the back of the book. Put these words in the sentences. Then answer the questions.

protest   rights   ordinary   empires   rulers

The year is 3010. There are no countries in the world. There are three big **a** ..... You are an **b** ..... person in the biggest empire. The people don't like the **c** ..... and are not free. You and your friends want to **d** ..... You want to fight for your **e** ..... You want to be free. Which of these things will you do?

- go on protest marches
- use violence
- use nonviolence
- break the law and go to prison
- try to move to a different empire

Do other students have the same answers?

2 Talk about Gandhi. What do you know about the man, his life, and his ideas?

3 Read the Introduction on page iv. Answer these questions.

   a Why did Gandhi start to fight for Indian rights in South Africa?

   b What was different about Gandhi when he arrived in India in 1915?

   c What new kind of protest did the world learn from Gandhi?

While you read

4 Two of these sentences are wrong. Which ones?

   a ..... Mahatma means "Great Soul".

   b ..... The British bought clothes and sugar in India.

   c ..... Indians worked in different countries in the British Empire.

   d ..... Gandhi and Kasturbai married when they were thirteen.

   e ..... Gandhi enjoyed London life.

   f ..... A South African policeman threw Gandhi off a train at Petermaritzburg.

   g ..... Gandhi read only holy books.

   h ..... Under the "Black Law", any Indians without papers went to prison.

   i ..... When the police hit Gandhi's protesters, the protesters did not fight them.

After you read

5 Answer these questions.

    a What two mistakes did Gandhi make when he was a young man?

    b How did Gandhi change when he was in London?

    c Why did Gandhi leave South Africa in 1914?

6 Work with another student. Have this conversation.

    Student A: You are Gandhi. Put your papers in the fire. Why are you doing this? Tell the policeman.

    Student B: You are a South African policeman. What is Gandhi doing? Ask him. Tell him about the law.

Chapters 3–4

Before you read

7 Look at the names of Chapters 3 and 4.

    a Why do you think Gandhi needs "to find India"?

    b Who do you think will "teach India a lesson"?

While you read

8 Underline the right words in *italics*.

    a Gandhi arrived in India in *ordinary / expensive* clothes.

    b Gandhi always traveled in *first / third* class.

    c *Soldiers / farmers* are in a higher Hindu class than *soldiers / farmers*.

    d Gandhi told the *Untouchable family / his wife* to leave the ashram.

    e On a "no-work day," children *do / don't* go to school and workers *do / don't* go to their offices.

    f The British shot *a small number / hundreds* of protesters in Amritsar.

    g The British sent Gandhi to prison for *violent / nonviolent* protest.

After you read

9 Discuss these questions with other students.

    a Can nonviolent protest work?

    b Can you think of any times in the past when it worked?

    c Is it a good way to protest?

Chapters 5–6

Before you read

10 Gandhi started ashrams in South Africa and India. He thought it was the best way to live. Would you like to live on an ashram? Why (not)?

While you read

11 <u>Underline</u> the mistakes in these sentences. Write the right word.

a Hindus and Muslims often fought in the country. ....

b Gandhi stopped his fast before the violence stopped. ....

c Gandhi doesn't see the children on the ashram every day. ....

d Indians didn't want to pay the British for water from India's oceans. ....

e Only Gandhi and Nehru went to prison after the Salt March. ....

f Things were better after Gandhi's visit to London. ....

After you read

12 Work with another student. Look at the magazine writer's questions on page 14. Change the questions and ask them about your life.

Student A: You are the magazine writer. You ask the questions.

Student B: You answer the questions.

Chapters 7–8

Before you read

13 Gandhi fasted many times in his life. Discuss these questions.

a Why did he fast? Was it a good idea?

b Do other people fast? Why do they do it? Does it help?

While you read

14 Who:

a went to the movies on the first day of Gandhi's fast in 1932? ....

b sat next to Untouchable children in school? ....

c wrote to Indian leaders in 1942? ....

d died in 1944? ....

e wanted two Indias? ....

f was the first leader of independent India? ....

g shot Gandhi on January 30, 1948? ....

After you read

15 Find the right word.

    a In 1936 Gandhi started a new ..... in Wardha.

    b Gandhi didn't like the ..... of Karl Marx.

    c Gandhi wanted India to give ..... to Pakistan.

    d Gandhi wasn't ..... on Independence Day.

    e The most important thing for Gandhi was ..... .

Writing

16 Look at the names of the chapters on page iii. What does each one mean? Write sentences. Example:

An ordinary boy: Gandhi was not born into an important family. He went to school and played in the streets with other ordinary boys.

17 There are different classes of Hindu in India. The Untouchables are the bottom class. Other classes do not like them. Are there groups in your country with this problem? Read about them, and then write about them.

18 You work for an English-language newspaper in India. It is January 31, 1948 and Gandhi is dead. What did Gandhi do for the people of India? Why was he important to them? Write about it for your newspaper.

19 Look at the rules for Gandhi's ashram on page 14. What rules do you follow in your life? Write some down.

20 A newspaper writer follows the Salt March. He/She asks a marcher questions. Write their conversation. Example:

Writer: How many kilometers are you walking today?

Marcher: I don't know, but my legs are very tired.

21 "Gandhi's life and ideas are still important today." What do you think—yes or no? Write your ideas.